365 Days
of
Family Fun

Charlotte Hopkins

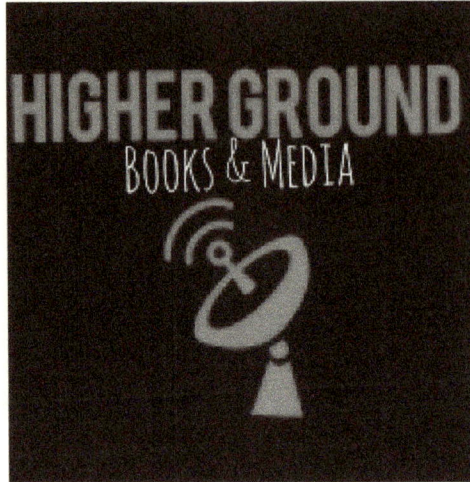

Higher Ground Books & Media
Springfield, Ohio.
http://highergroundbooksandmedia.com

Printed in the United States of America 2019

365 Days
of
Family Fun

Charlotte Hopkins

DEDICATION

I wrote this book with the hopes of creating family togetherness - to keep children happy, having fun – all year around!

This book is dedicated to my favorite children – Landen Sanner, Gavin Sanner, Kathryn Hopkins, Sidney Hopkins, Abby Anderson, Wyatt Anderson, Vickie Rubero, Raeden Plutt, Airalyn Plutt, Chazdine Harmon, Lydia Hott, and my newest favorite, Caiden Biddle.

And to my favorite teens - Robert Anderson, Eric Anderson, Tyler Pietschmann, Katrina Antill, Charlayne DeCecco, Roseanna DeCecco, and Releigh Clark.

A special thanks to Kellie Kurta, Stephen and Meg Hopkins, Ben and Lisa Leach, Terri Quick, Chuck and Christina David, and Charlotte Raschke for the photos that made my book cover extra special!

And as always, a very special dedication to – Justin, Megan, and Aubreyanna!

INTRODUCTION

Family fun and togetherness go hand-in-hand so get ready
to take off on 365 FUN filled days of adventures. These
unique ideas can be enjoyed by adults and children of all
ages. With a timeline of activities to enjoy – you can start
your countdown in June, in October, or on January 1st!

Put a spin on your summer vacation, with a
STAYCATION that will take you around the world. Make
new holiday traditions and enjoy days, such as, Sorry
Charlie Day, and Aquarium Month. These creative
activities will instill a lifetime of memories and even have
you giving back to your community in a whole new way.
The excitement begins now!

JANUARY

January 1: Make an "Adventure Box." Wrap up a shoe box using wrapping paper, brown paper, construction paper, even contact paper, as long as it is plain in color. Decorate the box using markers, stickers, decorations, decals, and more! Fill it with movie stubs menus and projects you make through the year. On New Year's Eve, empty it and see what awesome stuff happened that year!

January 2: Sew buttons and decals onto a plain colored tote bag. Draw designs with fabric markers. Use your new bag for the year of activities ahead. Before you begin your activities for the day, fill the bag with what you will need.

January 3: JRR Tolkien birthday is January 3, 1892. Celebrate by reading one of his books and watching The Hobbit.

January 4: Today is Trivia Day! Play trivia games with your friends! Play a game of "Fun Facts about Me" with your guests. Pass around a bowl of M&M's or Skittles. Tell them to take as many as they want but do not eat them yet. When they are done choosing, you can start your game. Tell them that for each piece of candy that they picked from the bowl, they have to tell something about themselves.

January 5: Celebrate National Bird Day by spending the day at the Aviary learning about the different birds. When you come home make a pine cone bird feeder to hang outside. Or you can roll toilet paper rolls in honey and then in bird seed. Attach a hook and hang it up for the birds. When you get home, watch the movie, Fly Away Home.

January 6: For Bean Day make a big bowl of homemade chili and play "Don't Spill the Beans!"

January 7: Spend the day volunteering at an animal shelter (and make plans to return)!

January 8: This is Hot Tea Month, sample a variety of flavored teas. Make a homemade book to describe the teas you tried and how you liked them. Glue pictures of the teas inside too. Your Tea Book can be the first addition to your Adventure Box. Here is another fun activity for the day. Cut out a tea cup or tea kettle from construction paper and staple on a tea bag. On your project write this poem:

I'll try my best in every way,
to be extra sweet each day.
But if I become sad and grumpy,
I'll relax and have a cup of tea.

January 9: Celebrate National Soup Month by creating your own specialty soup! End the day by reading the books, *Stone Soup, Duck Soup, The Cat Who Liked Potato Soup,* and *Pumpkin Soup.*

January 10: Start growing a houseplant or even a house garden in honor of Houseplant Appreciation Day!

January 11: Start keeping a journal – yes, even you guys can keep a journal. Ulysses S. Grant and Abraham Lincoln kept a journal! On your first page make a list of 10 things that you want to do in the year ahead.

January 12: The first public museum opened today on January 12, 1773, in Charleston, South Carolina. It was about the history of that region. Spending the day visiting a museum – or two! When you get home, watch Night at the Museum.

January 13: Learn about astrology, the different astrology signs and the meanings and stories behind them, even if it is only for entertainment.

January 14: Start a latch hook project – easy and fun!

January 15: For Bath Safety Month, go over the rules for being safe in the bathtub, like never reaching for the radio, no electrical appliances near the tub, and staying out of the bathtub when it is lightning outside! Did you know that a hairdryer can electrocute you if it falls into the tub – even if it is not plugged in? Here is a fun recipe for bath salts:

2 cups of sea salt
½ cup avocado oil
¼ cup apricot oil
squirt of honey
fragrance oil

Mix ingredients until desired consistency.

Or you can keep it simple and add food coloring to shaving cream/whipped cream; use a mixer to make it thick. Mix on low for 2 minutes. This will create paints for the bathtub! Use a cupcake pan as cups to hold your different colors.

January 16: Make puppets with paper bags and socks. Decorate with googly eyes and buttons and use yarn for the hair. Watch Pinocchio while you make your puppets.

January 17: Make a picnic basket! All that's needed here is a brown shopping bag, paper plates, glue and magazines. First cut the shopping bag in a horizontal direction; completely removing the top half. The bottom half will be the basket. Decorate the bottom half with paint, dabbers and markers. You can even add beads, foam shapes, lace and photos. From the top half that you removed, cut a long strip of paper to be used as the handle. Attach the handle with glue, staples or any type of fastener. Now it's time to "prepare" the food for the picnic. Cut pictures of food and drinks from the magazines and glue them to the paper plates. Make as many different plates as possible. Place the plates in the basket and you are ready for a picnic!

January 18: This is the birthday of A.A. Milne – the author of Winnie the Pooh! Make a bowl of popcorn and watch your favorite Winnie the Pooh movie! Now write your own stories about a friendly teddy bear.

January 19: For National Popcorn Day, sprinkle different flavors on homemade popcorn – like Ranch or Cinnamon Sugar. Also make popcorn balls for dessert! String popcorn and hang it outside for the birds to eat. You can also play the popcorn game: Place a piece of popcorn at the ends of a table for each of you. Using a drink straw, blow the popcorn to the other end of the table.

January 20: It is Penguin Awareness Day! Spend the day at the Aviary, learning about penguins (some will even let you feed them!). Also visit the home of the penguins at the zoo. End the day by watching the documentary, March of the Penguins.

January 21: Today is Martin Luther King Jr. Day! He is famous for his "I Have a Dream Speech. Talk about your dreams with your children. In your journal, title a page, "What I want to be," and write down everything they want to do as they grow up. Also, include things they want to invent, cars they want to drive, and places they want to go to.

January 22: Go sled riding and build a snowman! When you get home, warm up with hot chocolate and a grilled cheese sandwich. Still no snow? That's ok, build a fort and crawl inside to color winter pictures and read books. Don't forget your grilled cheese sandwich and hot chocolate! Add an extra sweet flavor by crushing a candy cane into powder and sprinkling it on your hot chocolate.

Whether you have snow – or no snow – enjoy a few games of Don't Break the Ice.

January 23: Spend the day baking cookies – peanut butter cookies, chocolate chip cookies, or sugar cookies – there are many types, have fun with it. You will need them for tomorrow's project. If you are worried about egg allergies, they can be substituted.

One egg can be substituted with one of these:

1/3 cup applesauce
¼ cup yogurt
½ mashed banana
¼ cup vegetable oil

January 24: It is Compliment Day! Gather your cookies and a stack of notepads and deliver a cookie, a packet of hot chocolate and a special note to friends, family, neighbors, and others in the neighborhood.

January 25: Start a new hobby for National Hobby Month...anything from model railroading, photography, painting writing, reading, animal rescue, couponing and more!

January 26: Celebrate Australia Day by learning about the country's history. Create an Australian dinner and watch Steve Irwin's movie, The Crocodile Hunter.

January 27: Make Monster Dip and scoop it up with crackers or pretzels. Munch on your Monster Dip while you watch, "Monsters Inc."

Monster Cookie Dough Dip

1 (8 ounce) package cream cheese, softened
½ cup butter, slightly softened
1 cup creamy peanut butter
2 cups powdered sugar
3 Tablespoons brown sugar
1/4 cup all-purpose flour
1 teaspoon vanilla
2 ½ cups rolled oats, old fashioned or quick (see Note)
2/3 cup plain M&Ms (give or take)
1 cup semi-sweet chocolate chips

With a hand mixer or stand mixer, beat the cream cheese, butter, and peanut butter until smooth. Add in the powdered sugar, brown sugar, flour, and vanilla. Mix in the oats. Add the M&Ms and chocolate chips.

January 28: Make pencil cups to store pencils and pens, utensils, paintbrushes, or to give as gifts. Decorate construction paper or contact paper and wrap it around clean tin cans. You can add stickers, gems, and lace. By the way, start saving up stickers, of all shapes and sizes, you will need them for an activity in September.

January 29: Happy National Puzzle Day! Start building a puzzle or play crossword word puzzles, word searches or Sudoku. Puzzles are a great way to exercise your mind! Did you know that Arthur Wynne is the Father of the Crossword Puzzle?

If you wooden puzzles with missing pieces then use the pieces that you have left to turn into magnets.

January 30: Make your own play-doh!

Play-Doh
1 cup flour
1 Tablespoon vegetable oil
1 cup water
1/3 cup salt
2 teaspoons cream of tartar
Food coloring (or Kool-aid)

Mix together all the ingredients, except the food coloring, in a 2 quart saucepan. Cook over low/medium heat, stirring. Once it begins to thicken, add the food coloring. Continue stirring until the mixture is much thicker and begins to gather around the spoon.

Remove the dough onto wax paper or a plate to cool. Add the food coloring and knead. You can also use Kool-aid for coloring   Store in Ziploc baggies.

January 31: Make a time capsule to be opened in 20 years. Include a list of things you want to accomplish! You can use a storage tote to make your time capsule and hide it either in the attic or deep inside your closet. Take photos of your children filling up the time capsule and lay the photos on top before you close the lid.

FEBRUARY (Don't forget to save stickers for September)

February 1: Have a magazine scavenger hunt! You will need a variety of magazines. First, make a list of items that you want the children to find. Second, let them search for those items in the pages of the magazines. These are examples of items to look for; feel free to add more words.

1) transportation (car, airplane, train)
2) animal
3) hot/cold drink
4) flower
5) something you write with
6) camera
7) sport
8) flag
9) person wearing gloves
10) necklace
11) someone talking on the phone
12) cartoon character
13) ice cream
14) animal that lives in the water
15) lamp
16) man/woman in a suit
17) fruit
18) tree
19) chair
20) baby
21) purse
22) umbrella
23) someone cooking
24) someone playing a musical instrument
25) fireman/police officer

February 2: Celebrate Groundhog's Day – Read children's books about Punxsutawney Phil and check to see if he saw his shadow this year! Write your own story of how Punxsutawney Phil will spend his special day. If he does not see his shadow then spend the day making an indoor vegetable garden. If he sees his shadow then spend the afternoon painting spring pictures. Also, make Snow Ice Cream as a treat!

Snow Ice Cream:

Ingredients

1-1/2 to 2 cups sugar, to taste
1 teaspoon imitation vanilla or 1/2 teaspoon real vanilla
1 quart heavy whipping cream or half-and-half
6 quarts clean, fresh snow (fluffy, not packed)

In a large mixing bowl, combine the sugar, vanilla, and whipping cream. Add snow, 2 cups at a time.

February 3: Today is "the day the music died." It marks the death of Buddy Holly, Richie Valens and the Big Bopper in a plane crash in 1959. Listen to the music of these 3 artists who helped build the cornerstone of the rock and roll kingdom! Have a day of music. Listen to different types of music – even ones that you never listened to before. You may just find a new interest!

February 4: Thank a Mailman Day! Do something special for your mailman – Make a jar of trail mix or present him/her with a mug and a packet of hot chocolate for the end of the workday! Read children's books, such as, The Jolly Postman, A Visit to the Post Office, Dear Peter Rabbit, and Amelia Writes Again. Have your child write letters to friends or family members and go to the post office to mail them.

February 5: For National Weatherman's Day, learn all the interesting facts about the weather, including natural disasters in history, such as the "Dust Bowl" of the Midwest. Make a bowl of popcorn and watch the Wizard of Oz.

February 6: Make a craft using plastic canvas.

February 7: This day, marks the day that the The Beatles came to America. Spend the day reading about the history of Beatlemania! Listen to Beatles music and spend the night watching Beatles movies. Have steak and coke for dinner. A favorite meal of the Beatles when they were on the road!

February 8: Make homemade Valentine cards and deliver them to a local nursing home.

February 9: Visit a community art museum and explore the different types of art. On your way home pick up poster boards for each of you to paint your own masterpiece!

February 10: It's Black History Month! Learn about the African American culture, including those who made a difference in the world.

February 11: For White T-Shirt Day, you will need a white shirt and fabric markers. Design a fun shirt for yourself and a friend.

February 12: Today is Abraham Lincoln's birthday! Build a log cabin from pretzel logs. Watch the You Tube video, "Abraham Lincoln Children's Tales, Stories and Fables." It is an 8 minute video by Muffin Stories. Also, start collecting pennies from businesses, neighbors, friends, and family for the rest of the month. On the last day of February donate the pennies to a Civil War group.

February 13: Make your own slipper socks by decorating the bottom of socks with puff paint.

February 14: Make friendship bracelets to remind those close to you how important they are! You can attach a key ring if you want!

February 15: Build a Gingerbread House and decorate with lots of gumdrops to commemorate National Gumdrop Day. To make it extra sturdy use a milk or juice carton as the base. Cut off or fold back the top to make it a complete rectangle. Cover it in frosting, then a layer of graham crackers and then decorations.

February 16: Make clay candy dishes and trinket bowls. Press gems, beads, and mosaic tiles, into the clay, before it hardens! You can make your own clay by combining 1 Cup of Corn flour, 2 Cups Bicarbonate Soda, and 1 ½ cups of water.

February 17: For Random Acts of Kindness Day, spend the day doing kind acts. Make your little corner of the world, a happy place today! Some suggestions:

*Take hot chocolate to a security guard.

*Leave flowers on a stranger's car at the grocery card with a note that says "Happy Random Acts of Kindness Day!"

*Put 6 quarters in an envelope and tape it to a vending machine with a note that says, "Please take this and enjoy a snack on me."

*Go out to lunch and give a compliment to the manager about your waiter/waitress.

*Buy a bunch of bananas and go to businesses to give a banana to a worker inside.

February 18: Celebrate President's Day by reading up on the lives of our presidents and even the first ladies! Some interesting books about the presidents are: Presidential Elections and Other Cool Facts by Syl Sobel and The New Big Book of U.S. Presidents: Fascinating Facts about Each and Every President, Including an American History Timeline. A good book about the First Ladies are Secret Lives of the First Ladies by Cormac O'Brien. Then make a collage of photos cut from magazines that remind you of the presidents that you just read about in those books. For the collage use construction paper or a poster board.

February 19: Have an afternoon of playing Yahtzee! It is a fun math game that teaches children to add quickly.

February 20: Learn needle point and make something to hang on your wall.

February 21: Make seed bead crafts. When they are done, apply double stick tape to display on shelves, walls and even your car dashboard.

February 22: Celebrate George Washington's Birthday with a homemade cherry pie, cherry cookies and cherry punch! Cherry cheesecake bites are a fun delicious treat for children. Have a bowl of cheesecake mixture and a bowl of either crushed (to a powder) cookie crumbs or graham crackers. First dip the cherries in the cheesecake and then into the bowl of graham cracker/cookie crumbs. While you eat your snacks, play Hi! Ho! Cherry-oh!

February 23: Play tennis (or badminton) in honor of Tennis Day! You can even play "indoor tennis." Glue large craft sticks to paper plates to make tennis rackets and for the tennis ball, use a balloon.

February 24: Visit the craft section of Target/Walmart and get material to design and make your own magnets. Hang a cookie sheet on the wall, to display your creations! You can even paint the cookie sheet your favorite color!

February 25: Spend the afternoon playing cosmic bowling. Pick up a plastic bowling set and create a bowling alley at home!

February 26: For "Tell a Fairy Tale Day," Read stories from Grimm's Fairy Tales.

February 27: Get a plain wooden box and fine tipped permanent markers and design something great!

February 28: Learn different facts about animals and watch fun animal movies, such as, Free Willy, Benji, Dr. Dolittle, and Cats & Dogs. Read book with fun loving animals characters, such as, Llama Llama, Pigeon, Paddington Bear, and The Story of Ferdinand. Here are some fun animal facts to get you started:

*Horses have better memories than elephants.

*Dogs make about 10 sounds and cats can make over 100 sounds. However, cats only meow to communicate with humans.

*Pigs are extremely intelligent. Piglets will run to the sound of their mother's voice and can recognize their name.

*Cows first came to America in 1611. Until the 1850's, every family owned a cow.

Play the fun animal games Hungry Hungry Hippo and Animoes.

February 29: This is Leap Day! It only happens every 4 years! On this day, read your favorite Frog and Toad books. Make Frog Log Mix by combining either lime Jello or lime sherbet mixed with green M&M's and Junior Mints. Watch a video with the most famous frog – Kermit the Frog! Color pictures of frogs while you go over Fun Frog Facts!

Did you Know.....

*Frogs don't drink water they absorb it through their skin.

*Frog bones form a ring when the frog is hibernating - just like trees do! Scientists can use these rings to figure out the age of a frog.

*You can often tell the difference between a male and female frog by the size of their eardrum, which can be seen behind their eyes. If the eardrum is smaller than the eye, the frog is a female. On males their eardrum is the same size as the eye.

*A group of frogs is called an "Army."

*Europeans used tree frogs to predict the weather. When they started croaking it meant it was going to rain.

MARCH (Don't forget to save stickers for September)

March 1: For National Pig Day, visit a local pig farm. Watch a Piglet cartoon, Miss Piggy and the Muppets movie or Babe. Compete in a fun game of Pop the Pig. End the day reading the Olivia books and The 3 Little Pigs.

Did you know that pigs are clean animals and prefer water to mud?

March 2: Today is Theodor Geisel's birthday – also known as Dr. Seuss Day! Yes, Dr. Seuss's real name is Theodor Geisel (pronounced the same as "diesel.") There are many ways to celebrate this special day! Start the day by reading the book *In a People House*. Take a walk through your house to see how many items you can find.

As you read *One Fish, Two Fish, Red Fish, Blue Fish* create a mixture of Rainbow Goldfish crackers and Puffy Goldfish crackers. Use ice cream cones as serving bowls.

On You Tube look up the video "Tim Tebow reads Green Eggs and Ham." Give a copy of the book for your child to read along.

After you read the *Cat in the Hat* make the hat for your child to wear. Cut strips of construction paper and attach to make a headband. Cut a rectangle from white construction paper and add red strips of paper.

Now make a snack of the Cat's hat! Start with a cracker and spread cream cheese on top. Add a slice of a cherry tomato, the cream cheese – repeat these steps to make your hat.

March 3: For Peach Blossom Day make homemade peach jam! If possible, plant a peach tree! Then enjoy the movie, James and the Giant Peach.

March 4: Make a homemade ring toss game. Cut the centers out of paper plates. Color them with markers and decorate them with decals and stickers. Use a paper towel tube as the pole for your ring toss game.

March 5: Organize a yard sale of all crafts for National Craft Month. Name it the "Craft Show Kickoff" and have your friends join you! Plan it for the last day of March! You can make key chains, jewelry, napkin rings, or even jars of trail mix.

March 6: Start a scrapbook celebrating your friends and family!

March 7: Make a collage. Here are 2 themes to choose from:

"From Here to There" - The children can search for pictures of any means of transportation. They can include everything from cars and trucks to horseback riding, snowmobiles and jogging.

"The Great BIG Outdoors" - In this collage there are so many types of pictures they can seek. These pictures can include trees, leaves, rocks, flowers, animals, lakes, waterfalls, grass, the sun, the moon and stars.

March 8: Enjoy the book, "If You Give a Mouse a Cookie" and then it's off to make a delicious cheese ball! Enjoy your cheese ball while you watch the beloved mouse movies Stuart Little and Mouse Hunt!

Here is an easy cheese ball recipe:

Ingredients:

16-ounce cream cheese (room temperature)
2 cups cheddar cheese
3 tablespoons minced onion (optional)
1 teaspoon ground cumin
2 cups Nacho Cheese chips, crumbled

In a mixer combine cream cheese, cheddar, onion, and cumin. Mix until creamy. Shape to form a ball. Chill for 2 hours. When ready to serve, roll ball into crushed nacho chips. Serve with chips, crackers, pretzels, and vegetables.

March 9: For Music in Our Schools Month, show your appreciation for the music teachers in your child's school by collecting a variety of music books and CD's and donating them to the music program at your child's school. Or you can make Mix CD's for them. You can also create your own music books by photos and typing music facts. Bind them together in a binder or folder.

March 10: This is Middle Name Appreciation Day! Get your journal and talk to others about what their middle name is and how their parents chose that name. Many have interesting stories behind their names.

March 11: Celebrate Johnny Appleseed Day by learning the story of Johnny Appleseed. Make homemade apple fruit snacks by freezing drop of applesauce to parchment paper. Also, make homemade applesauce.

4 Apples – peeled, cored, and chopped
¾ cup water
¼ cup white sugar
½ teaspoon ground cinnamon

In a medium saucepan combine apples, water, sugar, and cinnamon. Cover and cook over medium heat for 15-20 minutes, or until apples are soft. Allow to cool, then mash with a fork or potato masher.

March 12: Here is a recipe of an early girl scout cookie. Make these for Girl Scout's Day.

AN EARLY GIRL SCOUT COOKIE RECIPE

1 cup butter
1 cup sugar plus additional amount for topping (optional)
2 eggs
2 tablespoons milk
1 teaspoon vanilla
2 cups flour
1 teaspoon salt
2 teaspoons baking powder

Cream butter and the cup of sugar; add well-beaten eggs, then milk, vanilla, flour, salt, and baking powder. Refrigerate for at least 1 hour. Roll dough, cut into trefoil shapes, and sprinkle sugar on top, if desired. Bake in a quick oven (375°) for approximately 8 to 10 minutes or until the edges begin to brown. Makes six- to seven-dozen cookies.

For your boys, make a bowl full of dirt! Here is the recipe:

DIRT

Ingredients:

2 Cups Cold Milk
1 Pack (4 servings) Chocolate Pudding
1 8-ounce Cool Whip – thawed
1 Pack 16 Ounce Chocolate Sandwich Cookies (crushed)
Candy Worms, Flowers, Nut and Candy Frogs

Pour milk into large bowl and add pudding. Beat with whisk until well blended, 1-2 minutes. Let stand for 5 minutes. Stir in whipped topping and half of crushed cookies. For single servings, sprinkle 1 tablespoon crushed cookies in plastic cup. Fill with dirt mix. Decorate with nuts and candy!

March 13: For National Peanut Month, make homemade peanut butter, peanut butter cookies and even peanut butter dip:

Creamy Peanut Butter Dip:

2 tablespoons creamy peanut butter
1 tablespoon milk
½ cup whipped cream

In a small bowl, whisk together peanut butter and milk until combined. Gently fold in whipped topping. Serve with fruit and pretzels!

Fun Peanut Butter Facts:

*It takes about 540 peanuts to make a 12-ounce jar of peanut butter.

*By law, any product labeled "peanut butter" in the United States must be at least 90 percent peanuts.

*Two peanut farmers have been elected president of the USA – Thomas Jefferson and Jimmy Carter.

*Astronaut Alan Shepard brought a peanut with him to the moon. NASA astronauts think it's good luck to carry a peanut.

*There are six cities in the U.S. named Peanut: Peanut, California; Lower Peanut, Pennsylvania; Upper Peanut, Pennsylvania; Peanut, Pennsylvania, Peanut, Tennessee; and Peanut West Virginia.

*The Guinness Book of World Records reports that on April 3, 1973, Chris Ambrose, Clerkenwell, London, ate 100 peanuts singly in 59.2 seconds

March 14: Today is Learn About Butterflies Day. Learn the interesting facts about the butterfly. If the weather permits, plant a butterfly plant in your yard. Also, make a caterpillar from a cardboard egg carton. Cut the carton (egg side) in half, long ways. The end piece is the head of the caterpillar and the rest is the body of the caterpillar. Decorate with sequins, markers and more. If possible, put a butterfly plant in your yard. Don't forget to read "The Hungry Caterpillar."

March 15: For Potato Chip Day make your own potato chips and sprinkle with your own flavors! Did you know that potato chips were invented by Native Americans?

March 16: For Freedom of Information Day ask everyone you meet for interesting facts about America and why they love it here! Add them to your journal.

March 17: Celebrate St. Patrick's Day at a parade in the city. When you get home, cut out shamrocks from construction paper and decorate them with dabbers. Make shamrock cookies and top them off with green frosting and sprinkles. End the day by reading books, such as, "The Night Before St. Patrick's Day," by Natasha Wing and "Saint Patrick's Day," by Gail Gibbons. During Irish American Month, celebrate the history of the Irish!

March 18: Read the story of *The Last Unicorn*. Make a unicorn horn snack! Turn a sugar cone ice cream cone upside-down on a plate. Cover in vanilla frosting and sprinkle with rainbow jimmies. Use markers to color images of unicorns. Cut the unicorns out, laminate the pages and turn them into magnets.

March 19: Learn crocheting, during National Crochet Week. Make a scarf – and a pair of warm slippers!

March 20: Celebrate the first day of spring by walking through the neighborhood and taking lots of photographs! Make an album of seasonal photos and add this to your Activity Box. Later when you take you photos for summer, fall, and winter try to revisit the same places. It will be interesting to see how the environment changes.

March 21: For Fragrance Day make your own body scrub!

In a mixing bowl, combine 2 cups of raw sugar (it looks like brown sugar), ¼ cup apricot oil, ½ cup avocado oil, big squirt of honey and essential oils. Mix and fill into small jars!

Make your home smell delicious by boiling a pot of orange peels, mixed with a ½ teaspoon of cinnamon, over a medium heat.

March 22: Have a ducky day and learn all about ducks. Some fun books to read when you get home are *Make Way for Ducklings*, *The Story About Ping*. Younger children will enjoy playing Lucky Ducks.

Did you know?

A duck's feathers are waterproof.

The duck's feet have no nerves so they never get cold.

Ducks are divided into 2 groups – river ducks and sea ducks.

March 23: Make Easter Eggs out of construction paper or card stock. Design them and write inspirational thoughts. Delivering them to the children in Children's Hospital is tomorrow's activity. Also make "Crispy Easter Eggs" and deliver them to the children as well. To make Crispy Eggs, mix Rice Krispies, marshmallow cream, crushed M&M's and peanut butter (optional). Combine ingredients and make small eggs. Store the eggs in egg cartons.

March 24: Deliver the homemade Easter Eggs and Crispy Eggs to the children in the hospital.

March 25: Monkey around today with Curious George books! Bake banana cookies and blend delicious banana milkshakes. Enjoy your treats while you paint monkey pictures.

A favorite monkey song to sing has always been Five Little Monkeys Jumping on the Bed. Test your hand-eye coordination with a game of Barrel of Monkeys.

March 26: Today is Makeup Your Own Holiday Day! Choose a name and a theme for your special day! Choose the holiday menu and even design a holiday banner! Celebrate your new holiday every year!

March 27: Visit your local fire department. Meet the fireman and take photos of the trucks. Make "thank you" cards and a tray of brownies to leave with the firefighters.

March 28: For "Something on a Stick Day," Make breakfast kabobs for the morning. For lunch make fruit kabobs and corn dogs. For dinner make chicken and vegetable kabobs. Don't forget, toasting marshmallows on a stick at night!

For an afternoon activity, use a small box or carton to make a house with craft sticks. Color the craft sticks before you glue them onto your box/carton. You can also make bookmarks and puppets with craft sticks.

March 29: It's National Mom and Pop Business Owners Day, visit the local shops in your neighborhood. Talk to the owners about how they started and put their stories into a journal (or small notebook). At the end of the day write in your journal, what your business would be if you had your own.

March 30: Today is "National Take a Walk in the Park Day." Take your journal, camera, and brown bag and spend the day in the park. Take note of the things you see and learn. Collect flowers, leaves, stones and other interesting nature treasures that you find along the way.

March 31: Enjoy your craft show!

APRIL (Don't forget to save stickers for September)

April 1: April Fool's Day! Time to play jokes on our friends – be gentle – and be wary of those who don't have a big sense of humor!

April 2: Today is National Peanut Butter and Jelly Day! Taste the different peanut butters, including sunbutter, and the different flavors of jelly. You might find a new favorite. Use saltines to sample the different flavors.

Play the Peanut Butter and Jelly game. It's a fun card game where you try to build a peanut butter and jelly sandwich before a big fly lands on it!

Did you know that Grand Saline, Texas holds the title for the world's largest peanut butter and jelly sandwich weighing in at 1,342 pounds?

April 3: The first sundae was made on April 3, 1892 by John Scott, a Unitarian church minister, and Chester Platt, owner of Platt and Colt pharmacy. The flavors were Cherry Sunday, Strawberry Sunday and Chocolate Sunday. They were made with ice cream, cherry syrup and candied cherries. The name was changed to "sundae" 2 years later. Celebrate this day by having a "Make Your Own Sundaes" night at home!

April 4: For Library Week, take advantage of all of the services available at your library. If you don't have a library card yet, be sure to get one. Take note of upcoming events and be sure to attend.

April 5: On April 5, 1974, Stephen King's first book, Carrie, was released. The first link in a chain of hit movies and best sellers! Have a Stephen King marathon and discuss your favorite parts of the books. Later, try your hand at writing a scary story!

For younger children, have a Goosebumps marathon!

April 6: Today is "Sorry Charlie Day!" One of the most famous "Charlie's" is Charlie Brown. Have a marathon of Charlie Brown movies. Copy pictures of Snoopy and the Peanuts gang and color them with markers and colored pencils. Laminate them and use them as place mats or for mats on the top of your dresser.

At the end of this day, make 2 hard boiled eggs. Place one in a bowl of pop and one in a bowl of vinegar. Keep them in the refrigerator over night. They are for tomorrow's activity.

April 7: For this World Health Day there are fun games that teach a healthy lifestyle. Our Children are never too young to start that. First take the hard boiled eggs out of the refrigerator. The one soaked in vinegar shows the effect of too many potato chips on the enamel. The one soaked in pop shows the staining our teeth get from too much caffeine – pop, tea, or coffee. Then pass this egg around, taking turns brushing it with a toothbrush and toothpaste. This will show how clean our teeth can become if we brush our teeth daily.

Make a headband with strips of construction paper. Cut a circle from card stock or cardboard. Have your child wrap tin foil around the circle and attach it to the headband. Do not use staples, they get caught in the hair.

Set up a play doctor's office in your home with a scale, cotton balls, band-aids, gauze, and tiny flashlight. You can even make your own eye chart. Use dolls and stuffed animals as the patients.

Use black construction paper and Q-Tips to create an image of an x-ray of the arm and hand.

Read the books, *My Friend the* Doctor, and *The Berenstain Bears Go to the Doctor.* Then play a game of Operation!

April 8: During Garden Week plant flowers in your yard and in the yard of a single parent or an elderly neighbor.

April 9: Take a few guitar lessons to honor International Guitar Month. You can also learn about great guitarists, such as, George Harrison, Eddie Van Halen, and Jimmy Hendrix. Play the song written by Harrison, titled, "While My Guitar Gently Weeps."

April 10: Play a game of mini golf to celebrate Golfer's Day.

April 11: To celebrate National Submarine Day, visit the Soldiers and Sailors museum in Pittsburgh. When you get home watch the Beatles movie, "Yellow Submarine" and Don Knotts in The Incredible Mr. Limpet.

April 12: Think fast for the activities for these days. Start with playing the card game "War!" Play games that test your speed, such as, Perfection, Whac-a-Mole, and even Bop It. For older children the game, 5 Second Rule, will be a great challenge and a lot of fun!

Finish your day with reading, the Berenstain Bears book, The Big Road Race.

April 13: It's Scrabble Day! Have a Scrabble game day with your friends!

April 14: April Showers Bring May Flowers! Start a mini garden in plastic cups. In March, you can transfer your plants to the yard or to bigger flower pots.

April 15: The first McDonald's opened on April 15, 1955. Go through the drive-thru to pick up a McDonald's lunch and pay for the car behind you.

Here are a few Fun Facts about McDonald's to add to your journal:

*The first hamburgers cost 15 cents and the cheeseburgers were nineteen cents.

*Some of the first menu items include barbecue beef, chili, tamales, and a ham & baked beans meal.

*The first kid's meal was a peanut butter and jelly sandwich and french fries.

See if you can learn more fun facts to add to the list!

April 16: This is National Librarian Day! Do something special for your favorite librarian! Make them a gift bag with a book, tea bags, a mug, and cookies. Create a story book for your librarian! Staple pages together or use brass fasteners. Glue pictures to the pages and then write the words to the story underneath. Let your child take the story in any direction they choose.

April 17: For Daffy Duck's birthday, lay pillows and blankets on the floor and watch Looney Tunes cartoons - while you eat breakfast food!

April 18: For Newspaper's Columnists Day, start a newsletter at your place of employment or church. You can even start a family newsletter!

April 19: Paint ceramics! You can purchase small ceramics and paint at a craft shop.

April 20: In honor of National Poetry Month, read poems from Shel Silverstein to Edgar Allen Poe to Emily Dickenson. Practice your poetry skills. Write poems of different subjects and feelings! You might surprise yourself! Make limericks about your favorite places, food, and people. Make limericks about things that scare you, your favorite animals and hobbies, and places you want to travel to.

April 21: Sing your favorite songs to celebrate National Karaoke Week. Make mixed CDs, include a CD of holiday music.

April 22: This Earth Day, study some interesting facts about Mother Nature and save them in your journal. Also, take a walk in the park and collect plain colored rocks along the way. Take them home and paint them. Use a window box to create your own miniature rock garden!

April 23: During this Keep America Beautiful Month, clean up a local park or roadway.

April 24: This Administrative Professionals Day, prepare a fruit salad and a plate of different flavored crackers for your favorite office workers – either at your job, your doctor's office or even your bank!

When you get home make a corner of your room into an office.

April 25: For National Telephone Day, call family members that you have lost contact with through the years. Practice phone etiquette and how to call 911. Learn about Alexander Graham Bell and all of the changes of the phone from the beginning.

Fun Facts about the Telephone:

*The first phone call was for a call for help. Alexander Graham Bell spilled acid on himself and need Watson's help.

*The first cell phone call was made from the creator to his competitor to tell him that he completed the task of making the first cell phone.

*The camera phone was introduced to the world on a Siegfried and Roy commercial.

*Telephone service stopped for one minute during the hour of Alexander Graham Bell's funeral.

April 26: For National Pretzel Day, make homemade soft pretzels. You can twist your soft pretzels in the shapes of letters, as well. Here is a fun and easy recipe. Make chocolate covered pretzels and pretzel rods dipped in chocolate and candy pieces.

Soft Pretzels.

1 Package of Yeast
1 ½ cups of warm water
1 teaspoon salt
1 Tablespoon sugar
4 Cups flour
1 egg, beaten
rock salt/ sea salt

Preheat the oven to 350 degrees. Pour water into large bowl. Add yeast and stir until soft. Add salt, sugar, and flour. Mix and knead dough. Create shapes! Place on greased baking pan and brush with egg. Sprinkle with salt. Bake 12-15 minutes.

April 27: Today is Tell a Story Day! Try writing a children's book or your own fairy tale. Maybe put a spin on a classic fairy tale, or perhaps a sequel.

Children enjoy listening to audio cassettes/dvds while they read so make your own audio cassette/dvd. Read a story and record it at the same time. At a certain point your child can read a line. Have a cue for your child to follow so that when you point to them, they say, "time to turn the page!" Save the cassette/dvd so that they can listen to (and read along with)the story anytime! Make a copy (just to be safe)!

April 28: This is International Astronomy Day! Learn the facts about the planets and the interesting facts about our moon. You might be surprised at what you learn. Watch one or two of these movies - Armageddon, Apollo 13 and Space Cowboys.

April 29: Learn about the legend of the dragon and read fun books, such as, *When a Dragon Moves In*, *The Knight and the Dragon*, *My Father's Dragon*. Have fun with the Dragon Tales board game. And listen to the song, "Puff the Magic Dragon," while you paint pictures of dragons.

April 30: Today is National Honesty Day! Tell someone something that you have been holding inside for a long time. In your journal write secrets or questions that you would tell/ask certain people.

MAY (Don't forget to save stickers for September)

May 1: Volunteer for the week at Meals on Wheels.

May 2: Collect pillow cases and design them with markers or fabric paint and send them to our troops in Iraq and Afghanistan. They pass them on to wounded soldiers to store personal belongings during their hospital stays. If you send them early in the month they will receive them in time for Memorial Day.

May 3: For Foster Care Month, spend the day making necklaces and bracelets. Donate them to a foster care group in your area. Finish the day by watching the movie, Annie!

May 4: Have a chomping good time with alligators today. Start by playing Crocodile Dentist and a few rounds of Gator Golf. Sing, Five Little Monkeys Swinging from the Tree, and remember to read Zack's Alligator books and the book, *There's an Alligator Under My Bed*.

Make clothespin alligators. Paint a clothespin green, glue on googly eyes, and paint on teeth. And create an alligator swamp by filling a bin with shaving cream/whipped cream, that has been mixed with either green food coloring, green Kool-aid, or even green tempera paint. Gather plastic alligators to play in the swamp.

May 5: In honor of National Photograph Month, spend the day walking through town and your local park taking many photographs along the way. Take note of everything from the people to the petals on the flowers.

May 6: Celebrate Beverage Day! Set up an old fashioned lemonade stand! Finish the day off by reading *Lemonade for Sale*.

Have more fun with lemons by making Lemonade Art, here's what you will need – white paper, lemon juice and cotton balls. Draw a picture using the cotton ball dipped in lemon juice. Make sure your children know that they won't be able to see anything - yet. When you are done, set the papers out in the sun to dry. The lemon juice will turn brown from the heat and will show your "lemonade masterpiece."

May 7: Reconnect with your spiritual side. Start keeping a prayer journal.

May 8: Go horseback riding!

May 9: For National Train Day, take a train ride and visit a train museum! When you get home, watch The Polar Express!

May 10: Make this Old Stuff Day! Go to a nearby antique/thrift store and reconnect with the past. Pick your favorite item and start a collection!

May 11: For Twilight Zone Day, watch a Twilight Zone marathon with your friends.

May 12: Happy Mother's Day! A project for the special mom in your life – Make a candle for the special mom in your life. Draw words and images on wax paper. Wrap the paper around a pillar candle and heat it with a hair dryer until the image is transferred.

May 13: This is Police Week, do something special for your local police department. Color police images that you download from the internet. Laminate them and deliver them to the police. Treat them to a lunch of sandwiches and fresh fruit.

May 14: Lewis and Clark began their expedition on May 14, 1804. Their goal was to explore new territories. Take a note from them and visit a town that is new to you. Enjoy the shops and have lunch at one of their diners. Take lots of photos!

May 15: For Police Officer's Memorial Day, visit a Fallen Officer's Memorial. Learn more about the those on law enforcement, read *Everything You Wanted to Know about the Heroes in Blue*. A fun book for children to read is *A Day with Sergeant Rocky Bear* by Steven Whited.

To remember that being a police officer isn't all sadness, watch Police Academy.

May 16: Have a cook-out and invite the neighbors to celebrate National Barbecue Month. Bring out a Frisbee and a badminton set. It is also National Hamburger Month. Create your own special flavored hamburger with your homemade signature dressing to top it off.

May 17: Make "Cloud Dough" by mixing 8 cups of flour with 1 cup of baby oil or canola oil.

May 18: On Armed Forces Day write letters of thanks and encouragement and send them to military troop leaders in Iraq and Afghanistan. If you do not have an address to send them, then take the letters to your local VFW or American Legion. They will send the letters for you!

May 19: For Emergency Medical Services Week, have your church youth group, or local scout troop, make thank you cards and Rice Krispies treats for your local paramedics. Talk to your local fire department about a class on CPR and first aid. Have several friends and neighbors to join you in the class!

May 20: This is Pick Strawberries Day! Visit a working farm to pick your own fresh strawberries from their large garden. Or you can even start your own strawberry garden. Make strawberry pie, jelly or even smoothies!

May 21: For National Memo Day get Post-It Notes and leave messages all over for friends, family and co-workers. Pick up notepads and make a collection of "Top 10 Lists."

Ten Favorite Books
Ten Favorite Snacks
Ten Favorite Animals
Ten Favorite Cartoons
Ten Favorite Places to Visit

May 22: The last week before Memorial Day is National Backyard Games Week. Have a day of playing Frisbee, jumping rope, soccer, and kickball! Have lots of freeze pops and bottles of water on hand! Fill a bucket with ice to store your freeze pops. Make Kool-Aid ice cubes to go with your glasses of cold water.

May 23: Have fun with turtles today – it's World Turtle Day! Visit the aquarium at the zoo and take lots of photos of the turtles. At home, make a turtle using a paper bowl. Decorate the back of the turtle with paint, markers, or cut up pieces of construction paper. Make the head, tail and legs from construction paper and glue them to the underside of the turtle.

Enjoy watching the Ninja Turtles movie and the cartoon, *A Turtle's Tale*. Some fun turtle books to read include *Franklin*, *Yertle the Turtle*, and *I'll Follow the Moon*. Save fun turtle facts in your journal. Here are a few to get you started.

*Turtles smell through their throats.

*Sea Turtles can travel up to 10,000 miles in a year.

*Turtle eggs look just like ping pong balls.

*Turtles in South America make yelping sounds like a dog.

May 24: Attend a play at the Elizabeth Grand Theatre.

May 25: Have fun with marbles. Cut a pool noodle in half (length ways) to create a marble track. Practice shooting marbles and you can even bowl with marbles – use erase tops as bowling pins.

Make a marble painting using a shoebox, marbles, and paint. Cover the bottom of the shoebox with white paper. Roll the marbles in different paint colors, covering them in paint. Place the marbles in the shoebox and rock the box back and forth to create your masterpiece.

Make a snack of "Marbled Eggs." Make hard boiled eggs and roll them around to crack the shells. Place in a bag with a mixture of food coloring and 1 teaspoon vinegar. Keep refrigerated for 30 minutes. Peel the shelves and enjoy!

May 26: This is National Paper Airplane Day. Practice all the ways to make paper airplanes. You can also volunteer at a nearby daycare/ preschool to read a book about airplanes, such as, The Jet Alphabet Book by Jerry Pallotta, The Little Airplane by Lois Lenski and The Big Book of Airplanes by Caroline Bingham. Follow it up with an afternoon of making paper airplanes with the children.

May 27: For Memorial Day, visit either a memorial battlefield or a military museum.

May 28: This is National Bike Month, take a ride along the trails. When you get home, get a bucket of soapy water and wash it all over, like you would your car.

May 29: Take a boat ride. Remember to take plenty of photos of the water and the shore from afar.

May 30: Create a boat of your own today. Use a paper milk/juice carton. Cut one of the sides off and decorate inside with seats made from blocks, decorations and even make a captain's wheel with pieces of straws.

May 31: Make macaroons to celebrate National Macaroon Day. Add flavors to make chocolate and even banana.

JUNE (Don't forget to save stickers for September)

June 1: Ghostbusters movie premiered today in 1984. Make lime Kool-aid and snack on "slimed popcorn" while you enjoy the movie. Make this by melting white chocolate and adding green food coloring; then coating popcorn with your melted green chocolate. Also, make your own slime.

June 2: Celebrate National Fresh Fruit Month and plant a watermelon garden. Gather different fruits, juice drinks and a big bowl of ice to experiment and make fruit smoothies! Add sorbet or frozen yogurt if desired. Make a tray of fresh fruit and use yogurt as a dip. Use an ice cream cone as a personal serving bowl of fruit pieces.

Another great snack for National Fresh Fruit Month is fruit pizza!

Ingredients

1 package/tube sugar cookie dough
1 block cream cheese, softened
1 tub frozen whipped topping, thawed
1/2 cup powdered sugar
1 tsp. vanilla
6 strawberries
2 kiwi
1/2 cup fresh blueberries
1 can peaches in syrup

Preheat oven to 325. Bake sugar cookies for 10-12 minutes. Remove and cool for 10 minutes.

Whisk together cream cheese, vanilla and powdered sugar. Gently fold in whipped topping. Place 1/2 of mixture piping bag. To make a piping bag, put mixture in Ziploc bag and snip off the corner.

Wash and dry fruit and be sure to remove the stems from the strawberries. Peel the kiwi and slice both kiwi and strawberries. Drain peaches and slice them into chunks.

Place cookies on serving tray. Pipe filling onto each cookie and then top with fruit pieces. Refrigerate until needed - not more than 12 hours as the cookies will get soggy.

June 3: Spend the day painting and coloring! Use colored pencils, crayons, markers, paint, and even rubber stamps! You can make your own rubber stamps by sticking foam stickers to lids and bottle caps. Use white paper, coloring pages, construction paper and even pages from a coloring book. Save them in a scrapbook titled, "Artists at Work." Make it even more creative by making your own paint:

½ teaspoon Salt
Food Coloring
2 Cups Cold Water
3 Tablespoons Sugar
½ Cup Cornstarch

Combine all ingredients together and mix with a whisk until warm and thickens.

Have fun reading *Harold and the Purple Crayon*.

June 4: Attend a Mystery Dinner Theater. For younger children watch Blue's Clues and set up your own Blue's Clue's game at home! Play the board game, Clue, to test your detective skills. Finish the day by watching "Clue," the movie.

Make your own fingerprint pieces (that you can turn into ornaments or even charms for necklaces or keychains). Mix 2 cups of flour and 1 cup of salt. Gradually add water until it has the consistency of play-doh. Make an imprint of your fingerprint and create a loop at the top to make your creation into a charm. Bake at 250 degrees for 2 hours. After it cools completely, spray with a metallic paint.

June 5: Make homemade doughnuts to commemorate National Doughnut Day (the first Friday of June). Your children will enjoy the book, *Arnie the Doughnut*, by Laurie Keller. Remember to stop by Dunkin Donuts for your free donut!

June 6: For National Trails Day, take a walk along the trails! Skip rocks in the creek. Pack a picnic lunch for the afternoon!

June 7: For Dairy Month, visit a nearby dairy farm. Learn to make homemade butter and cheese.

Make Ooey Gooey Milk Paint by pouring condensed milk in several cups and adding food coloring to each one. Paint pictures of cows while you watch Charlotte's Web movie.

June 8: Spend the day at an amusement park.

June 9: For Aquarium Month, visit the aquarium at the Pittsburgh Zoo. When you get home watch, Finding Nemo, while you snack on Goldfish crackers and Swedish Fish. Finish the day reading *The Rainbow Fish*.

June 10: Celebrate Iced Tea Day by making a variety of flavored teas and cocktail sandwiches. Fun games to play today are Pretty Pretty Princess or Cranium.

Pineapple Iced Tea:

1 Quart Water
7 Tea Bags
1 Cup Pineapple Juice
2 Tablespoons Sugar

Boil water. Remove from heat. Add tea bags, cover and steep for 3-5 minutes. Discard tea bags and stir in pineapple juice, lemon juice and sugar; until sugar dissolves. Best if refrigerated overnight.

June 11: Jurassic Park premiered on this day in 1993. Celebrate dinosaurs by visiting the dinosaur display at a history museum.

Make a poster of dinosaur tracks. Set out several different paint colors and with different dinosaurs, dip their feet in the paint and make tracks across the paper. Frame your art and hang it on your child's wall.

Finish the day off by making a big bowl of popcorn and watching the Jurassic Park movie.

June 12: Dinosaurs are so much fun – extend the dinosaur excitement into 2 days! Make a batch of salt dough to create your own fossils.

2 Cups Flour
1 Cup Salt
¾ Cup Water
Plastic Dinosaurs

Mix the flour and salt. Gradually add the water, stopping when the mixture forms a dough. Form balls of dough and dust with flour. Knead the dough, adding more flour if the dough gets sticky. Flatten each ball of dough and cut circles using a cookie cutter, lid, can, or any round shape that you have on hand. Press the plastic dinosaurs into the dough to form imprints. Bake at 200 degrees for 2 – 3 hours.

Fun dinosaur movies to enjoy today can be, The Land Before Time, Barney, and Ice Age: Dawn of the Dinosaurs. End your Dinosaur Days by reading, *Danny and the Dinosaur* and *How do Dinosaurs Say Good Night*.

Fill pages in your journal with fun dinosaur facts.

*Dinosaurs lived on all of the continents. They became extinct 65 million years ago when a meteorite hit the Earth.

*Dinosaurs were first studied and named in 1824. The first was named, Megalosaurus. The word "dinosaur" means "terrible lizard" and was coined by Paleontologist Richard Owen in 1842.

*Roy Chapman Andrews found the first dinosaur nest in 1924. Before then, paleontologists were unsure how dinosaurs were born. Some dinosaur eggs are as big as basketballs.

*Othniel Marsh named one of his dinosaur discoveries, the Apatosaurus. He named another of his discoveries the Brontosaurus. However, he later realized that the Brontosaurus was actually the Apatosaurus, grown up.

*There are 930 types of dinosaurs. They range from the same size as a chicken – to as tall as 2 or 3 giraffes and the length of several school buses. Most were the size of an average adult.

*Mary Anning was one of the greatest paleontologists but didn't receive recognition for her discoveries until 2010 – because she was a woman. She used to hang off the edge of the Blue Lias cliffs to dig for fossils. She did this mostly in the winter because that was when the most landslides occurred, exposing fossils lost beneath the ground. One of her discoveries from the cliff included the Ichthyosaur.

June 13: To honor Adopt a Cat Month, go back to the pet shelter that you volunteered at on January 7th and spend the day, helping around the kennels. Again, make plans to go back! If possible, adopt a cat of your own! Read the exciting *Pete the Cat* books, along with *If You Give a Cat a Cupcake*.

June 14: Make a Flag Banner for the troops to celebrate Flag Day. Take a flat bed sheet, sew a small/medium flag into the middle. Gather together different colored sharpies and collect messages on your Flag banner, from people all over the neighborhood. Mail the banner to a military base here in America or to the troops overseas.

June 15: Spend the day at the arboretum and visit the Octopus Garden in the town of Friendship! On the way home listen to the Beatles sing "Octopus's Garden."

Make octopus snacks for lunch. Cut hot dogs into 1" pieces and insert spaghetti noodles (the hot dog piece should be in the middle). Bring to a boil and enjoy your octopus snacks!

June 16: Happy Father's Day! Make a stepping stone paperweight for the dad in your life. Mix ½ cup salt, ½ cup flour, and ¼ cup of water. Knead until dough forms. Roll flat and make impression of your foot. Bake at 200 degrees for 3 hours.

Challenge your dad to a game of Don't Wake Daddy.

June 17: For National Veggies Day, stop by a farmer's stand for fresh vegetables and onto Triple B to pick your own Cucumbers and green beans. Slice up your favorite veggies, get a variety of dressings and spend the day writing about your favorite memories. Watch Veggie Tales movies and read Peter Rabbit books (the famous carrot thief!).

June 18: This is Go Fishing Day, so spend the day at your favorite fishing spot. If you have never been fishing then make this the day that you learn.

At home, play the game Go Fishin' and the card game "Go Fish!"

June 19: Have a buggy day. Learn the different facts about bugs! Write you favorite insect facts and stories in your journal. Play buggy games "Cootie" and "Ants in the Pants."

Mix lemonade and blue Kool-aid to create your own bug juice. Serve them with a plate of "bugs on a log." To make those, fill celery sticks with either cream cheese or peanut butter. Then place raisins on top to symbolize the "bugs." Snack on your "bugs on a log" while you watch "A Bug's Life!"

Make worm tracks! Lay a piece of paper on a tray. Use a golf ball to cover in paint for your creation. Put the golf ball on the tray and rock the tray back-and-forth and up and down to create a trail of worm tracks!

June 20: Celebrate the beginning of summer by revisiting the places that you took your spring photos and take news ones. Add them to your album of seasonal photos.

June 21: Go roller skating for Go Skate Day!

June 22: Celebrate Rose Month by planting a rose bush in your yard. Have a red fruit salad for lunch that includes cherries, watermelon, strawberries, red grapes, raspberries and papaya. Snack on red licorice while you read the *Little Red Hen* and *Llama Llama Red Pajama*.

For dinner, have red pancakes (with the help of red food coloring) and cherry juice for dinner!

June 23: Make healthy Popsicles by freezing fruit juice in an ice cube tray or Dixie Cups. Insert the Popsicle stick after they have been in the freezer for 45 minutes. While you are waiting for your Popsicles to freeze, have fun outside with squirt guns and water balloons!

Another healthy snack for the day is yogurt bites. Fill ziploc baggies (halfway) with yogurt. Snip the corner of the bag. Pipe dots onto a nonstick tray and freeze.

June 24: For Swim a Lap Day, spend the day at the pool or at the water slides.

June 25: Today is Eric Carle's birthday, celebrate this day by reading his books *Brown Bear Brown Bear What Do You See*, *Polar Bear Polar Bear What Do You Hear*, *Today is Monday* and *Dragons Dragons*.

Mix coffee grounds with brown paint and paint pictures of brown bears. When the paint dries add the eyes. Learn about the different bears – where they live, what they ate and who their friends and enemies are.

Make a black spider as in his book, *The Very Busy Spider*. Paint a paper plates black and use either black strips of paper or black pipe cleaners to make the legs. Lay wiggly eyes on the plate before the paint dries.

June 26: It's Candy Month! Learn how to make homemade taffy! Visit a nearby candy store. A fun snack today would be an ice cream cone filled with mini marshmallows or M&M's. Also make a bowl of Snickers Dip. Serve with pretzels and enjoy while you read *The Candy Factory Mystery* and *The Giant Jelly Bean Jar*.

Snickers Dip

1 -2 blocks of cream cheese, 8 oz softened
8 oz. container of cool whip
¼ cup brown sugar
4 regular sized Snickers bars, cut into small pieces with the Crinkle Cutter

Mix the first 3 ingredients together and then add the Snickers.

Continue your candy celebration by playing a few games of Candy Land. Play a games of Candy Memory too. To play Candy Memory, get Styrofoam or colored plastic cups and arrange them in rows like you would with a deck of cards. Put a piece of candy under each cup. For each match they make, they get to keep the candy.

June 27: Build a village of Legos. Use a Mega Lego (or 2) to create Lego Jello. Make Lego cookies but cutting sugar cookies into squares and rectangles and using M&M's to decorate the notches on top. Enjoy your snacks while you watch the LEGO movie.

June 28: Play a few games of Dominoes. Get tricky and build a path of dominoes, as well.

June 29: Spend the day at the beach, collecting seashells and building sand castles.

Create a beach snack to enjoy when you get home. Fill a clear plastic cup ¾ full with blue Jello. When the blue Jello is partially set, drop a few gummy fish inside. Top with vanilla or banana pudding. Add a paper umbrella and 2 or 3 gummy bears.

June 30: Let the "beach day" continue with an "Under the Sea Day!" Lay beach towels out in the living room and watch The Little Mermaid. Play a few games of Shark Mania! Paint ocean pictures and make seashell necklaces. For lunch use cookie cutters to make fish shaped sandwiches.

Make a "Summer Beach Mix" by combining dried fruit (bananas, cherries, or cherries), popcorn, Raisinettes or yogurt flavored raisins, pretzels, and your favorite cereal. Substitutions for the snacks that you don't like can be: Chocolate Chips, Puffed Rice, Chex Cereal, Golden Grahams, Lucky Charms, Mini Marshmallows, Teddy Grahams, Goldfish Crackers. Serve your Summer Beach Mix from a beach pail and use the shovel as a scoop.

<u>JULY</u> (Don't forget to save stickers for September)

July 1: Bake muffins and visit our soldiers at the VA Hospital. Spend the day with them, listening to their stories. Write about it in your journal and share your experience with everyone!

July 2: Enjoy the afternoon at the Regatta!

July 3: Decorate for Independence Day! Make a wreath by cutting out the center of a sturdy paper plate and decorating in an Americana theme. Make a patriotic windsock, using a paper towel roll and red, white and blue paint and streamers! Make flash cards filled with American history questions. Jot down your favorite Americana facts in your journal!

July 4: For lunch, make star shaped cookies, that you decorate with frosting and sprinkles. Use the cookie cutters to make star shaped sandwiches. Enjoy your snacks while you watch, The Patriot with Mel Gibson. In the evening be sure to watch a fireworks show! Enjoy your Independence Day!

July 5: Check for nearby carnivals and spend the day having fun!

July 6: It's National Fried Chicken Day! Get creative and make a new fried chicken dish.

July 7: Bake a chocolate cake for Chocolate Day. For an extra fluffy cake, whip the eggs on high for 3 minutes before you add them. And add the oil last! For a recipe that calls for you to flour the bottom of your pan, use dry cake mix instead. The fun part will be decorating the cake when it's done! Use candy pieces coconut flakes and sprinkles. Don't forget a cold glass of chocolate milk. Enjoy your cake while you read *Curious George Goes to a Chocolate Factory* and watch Willie Wonka and the Chocolate Factory.

July 8: Have a day of sports! Learn about the different sports and play a few of them in the backyard or at the park. If you can't get out to play the sports, watch a few games on tv or the computer. Try to watch as many different ones that you can!

July 9: Have a Luau at home! Wear flower leis and dance to Hawaiian music! Play a game of Limbo and practice your "hula." Play coconut bowling by filling pop bottles – halfway – with colored water. Those are your bowling pins. Use a coconut as your bowling ball. Go to the library and learn fun facts about Hawaii and save them in your journal. End the day watching
Lilo and Stitch!

July 10: This is Teddy Bear Picnic Day! Have a picnic in the living room with your children, with your favorite teddy bears, crackers, juice, and sandwiches! Read Berenstain Bear books and load up on markers to color teddy bear pictures. Download pictures from Google images.

July 11: For Cheer Up the Lonely Day, spend the day visiting the elderly in nursing homes. Help them write letters to family members or to our troops overseas. Have lunch, sing songs and even make crafts or play Bingo!

July 12: Make a bumblebee craft. First by cutting out a bee hive from yellow paper – Long and round on one side and flat on the other side. Use a piece of sponge to dab into paint and create your honeycomb design on your beehive. Make a batch of honey cookie or cupcakes to enjoy while you watch the Bee Movie.

Teach your children the song, "Bringing Home a Baby Bumblebee." Also, listen to the Flight of the Bumblebee.

July 13: Celebrate Embrace Your Geekness Day with a Big Bang Theory Marathon or Revenge of the Nerds movies. Surf the web for your new favorite websites. For teenagers, check out ivillage and for younger children check out abcmouse.com.

July 14: Today is Cow Appreciation Day. Learn about the different cows and visit a farm to take photos of their cows! Jot down all your new facts in your journal. Watch the adventures of Otis the cow in the movie, Barnyard! You can also watch, Oh Brother, Where Art Cow?

Visit your local Chick-fil-A for fun cow activities!

July 15: Have a variety of pudding flavors to celebrate Tapioca Pudding Day! Along with tapioca pudding, make chocolate, vanilla, and even pistachio puddings! Have a picnic with your sweet treats. Use graham crackers and Nilla wafers to scoop up the pudding. End the day with backyard painting. Fill spray bottles with washable paint and spray your paint onto poster boards.

July 16: Spend the day riding paddle boats.

July 17: For Peach Ice Cream Day, spend the day peach-picking at either a working farm or a local farm stand. Use your peaches to make homemade peach ice cream. Then make peach sundaes and peach milkshakes. Sit back with your frozen treats and watch, "James and the Giant Peach!"

July 18: Decorate a large metal can with contact paper or felt. Add stickers, gems, lace and more. Use this to store your items in tomorrow's Scavenger Hunt.

July 19: Have a scavenger hunt. Step one: Get a gift bag and everyone puts one or two nice inexpensive items into it. Step two: Make a list of unusual items to seek. Step three: Give yourselves a time limit to find the sorted products – keeping in mind, these can be found or given items only, nothing can be bought. Step four: The winner gets the gift bag! In the event of a tie, the names go into a hat and the name chosen is the winner. Step five: Have fun! Remember, this is just a game! Use the can you decorated the day before to store your findings during the game.

July 20: Today is Moon Day! Have some night time fun! Catch lightning bugs in an old butter bowl. Remember to cut air holes and put grass inside. Be sure to let them go at the end of the night. Also, get some glow sticks and cut them open; pouring the solution into bottles of bubbles. This will make glow-in-the-dark bubbles. For night time bowling, pour a little sand into an empty pop bottle, then put in a glow stick! Have a midnight picnic under the stars while you read, Goodnight Moon!

July 21: Celebrate National Ice Cream Month by hosting an event at your local library or bookstore. Read a book for the children and bring ice cream and a great sweet collection of toppings, including candy, chocolate chips, crushed pretzels and fruit pieces, such as, cherries, strawberries and coconut. Avoid bringing peanuts because it is a common and dangerous allergy with children today. Choose one of these books to read: Max Drives Away by Rosemary Wells or Babe Ruth and the Ice Cream Mess by Dan Gutman

July 22: Make Fluffy Stuff! Mix 2 boxes of cornflour and one can of shaving cream. Add Kool-aid or powdered paint to make colors.

July 23: Olympics Day is celebrated in 160 countries. Create you own Olympics Games at home. Start the day by lighting the torch. Do this by making a torch using a paper towel tube with red and orange tissue paper sticking out to indicate a flame. Use tennis balls for the Shot Put. And use straws for a javelin throw. Stuff a tennis ball into an old sock to play Hammer Throw.

In your journal, add fun facts about the Olympics. Did you know???

The Olympics started in 776 BC and was initially a religious festival.

Olympics, as we know it, with races and games began in 1894 and the first place winners received a silver medal and an olive branch. The gold, silver, and bronze medals were not awarded to Olympic champions until 1904.

July 24: Enjoy creating chalk art! Use chalk to color images on construction paper and even on the sidewalks. You can even play a game of hopscotch! Make a tic tac toe board with chalk also. To make the game more tricky, use frisbees or bean bags.

Make sidewalk chalk paint by mixing 2 Tablespoons of corn starch, 4 Tablespoons of water, and 6 – 8 drops of food coloring.

July 25: For Threading the Needle Day learn to make crafts with just thread and fabric!

July 26: Attend a Kid's Workshop at Home Depot. They are held on the first Saturday of each month.

July 27: Spend the day playing with Matchbox cars at home. Use colored tape to make the outlines of roads. Use paper cups to make a garage. Fill a bin with soapy water to create a car wash. Use toilet paper tubes (glued together) or a manilla folder, taped to the floor, to create a garage.

July 28: Bake muffins and visit our soldiers at the VA Hospital. Spend the day with them, listening to their stories. Write about it in your journal and share your experience with everyone!

July 29: For National Hotdog Month, have a cookout and serve hot dogs with a wide variety of toppings. But hotdog shaped gum and even deliver some hotdogs to your local firefighters, paramedics and police officers!

July 30: Read the books *The Biggest Bear* by Lynd Ward and *Goldilocks and the Three Bears*. Make this a day to teach stranger danger and what to do if they find themselves lost.

July 31: Get a paint-by-numbers kit and have fun painting!

AUGUST (Don't forget to save stickers for September)

August 1: To celebrate National Raspberry Cream Pie Day, pick up fresh raspberries from a farmstand and make a Raspberry Cream Pie! Enjoy your pie while you read the book, "Jamberry."

August 2: The first Sunday in August is Friendship Day! Host an afternoon brunch for several friends and gift them with small goodie bags! End the day with a movie. Here are a few ideas:

UP
Stand By Me
Under the Tuscan Sun
My Best Friend's Wedding
Sisterhood of the Traveling Pants

August 3: It's National Watermelon Day! With the watermelons that you planted in June, enjoy slices or chunks of fresh watermelon. Make watermelon pie, watermelon jello, watermelon cupcakes and watermelon drinks – juice, smoothies and slushies!

August 4: Have fun learning about owls on this International Owl Awareness Day. Color pictures of owls with homemade swirly crayon melts. To make swirly crayon melts, place a few broken unwrapped crayons in cupcake wrappers. Put a few different colors in each one. Warm in the oven at 180 degrees. They only need to be in there for a few minutes because they melt fast. A few minutes after you remove them from the oven play the cupcake tray in the freezer for approximately 20 minutes.

This will make it easier to remove the crayons.

Read fun books about owls, such as, *Wow said the Owl*, *Oola the Owl Who Lost Her Hoot*, and *The Littlest Owl*.

Fun owl facts

*Owls are farsighted.

*There are more than 200 types of owls.

*Owls have 4 toes – 3 in the front and 1 in the back.

*An owl has a flat face and can turn its head 270 degrees (that's ¾ of a full circle).

August 5: Today is Work Like a Dog Day but instead of working like a dog – work with the dogs and revisit the animal shelter you volunteered at earlier this year. Bring a bag of kibble and dog treats and help out for the day.

August 6: For Wiggle Your Toes Day, treat yourself to a pedicure or give yourself a pedicure at home! Create a foot bath by filling a small bin with warm water and mixing in ¼ cup of Listerine and ¼ cup of vinegar. Soak your feet for 10 minutes.

August 7: This is National Lighthouse Day! Learn about the history of the lighthouses. Study their landmarks, heritage and beauty!

August 8: Today on this, Sneak Some Zucchini Onto Your Neighbor's Porch Day, get ready to deliver Zucchini friends to the people next door! Get creative and include a small foil bread pad, a decorative wooden spoon and recipes for zucchini bread and fried zucchini!

August 9: It is Book Lover's Day! Visit a small used book shop and rediscover treasured books of yesterday. Make a reading corner anywhere in your home. Stock it with books by your favorite author! If you don't have one, then find one. Here are some suggestions: Dean Koontz, Stephen King, Mary Higgins Clark, Jodi Picoult and Kristin Hanna.

Here are some options for your children: The Berenstain Bears, Amelia Bedilia, Holly Hobbie, Peter Rabbit and Eric Carle

Here are some options for your teens: Harry Potter, Judy Blume, Nancy Drew, RL Stein, and Suzanne Collins

August 10: Mmmm! It's National S'mores Day! Visit a nearby bookstore and hold a story hour for the children. Read a book about camping and then make s'mores! You can toast the marshmallows in the microwave.

August 11: Have a Staycation with your children or nieces and nephews. This is a vacation you take at home! On this Day one, choose a destination, such as, Ireland (you can pick any country). Prepare for your staycation by decorating a room with photos of where you will be visiting. Make homemade airline tickets. Find out how long it would take to travel there. And watch a movie or documentary about that country.

August 12: The next day, learn about the landmarks and culture.

August 13: On Day 3, study the history and battles of that country. Learn about their flag – how the colors and design was chosen. Make a flag representing that country and hang streamers of the same color as that country's flag.

August 14: For this part of the Staycation, cook food that is eaten in that country.

August 15: On this day, learn the history of the language spoken in that country. Teach yourself some of their words.

August 16: The Staycation is almost over. Today go to the library and look up some books on the country you chose. Learn some fun facts of that country.

August 17: On this last day, invite friends over for a meal of food eaten in that country and teach your friends, everything that you learned!

August 18: Visit the planetarium to learn more about the planets and the Milky Way.

August 19: Celebrate Aviation Day by spending the afternoon watching the airplanes depart and land at the airport.

August 20: It's almost Back to School time for many people! Have a movie marathon with those returning to school! Watch movies like, The Perfect Score, Back to School, Accepted, School of Rock and Orange County! Bring out the trivia cards that you made on January 4th and quiz each other. Walmart has one-subject notebooks on sale, pick some up for today's craft.

Decorate the notebook covers with drawings, stickers and more! Deliver them to friends or to children in the hospital.

August 21: For Zombie Awareness Day, wear your gray clothes (their chosen color) and visit the Zombie museum in Evans City. End the day with the movie that started the trend, "Night of the Living Dead." Visit the farm where the film was made. If you want something funny to watch, "Shaun of the Dead" would be just what you need!

Play a few games of Zed the Zombie.

August 22: Visit a laser tag center.

August 23: Fly a kite for Ride the Wind Day!

August 24: Have a UFO Day, with a movie marathon featuring Signs, They Live, Independence Day and ET. Even Marvin the Martian would be fun to watch today! Also, watch a documentary on UFO's to find out why so many believe in the concept.

August 25: This is National Be Kind to Humankind Week. Everyday this week, do at least one random act of kindness. For Day One, invite friends over for a day of playing BINGO. Make it more fun by offering small gifts for the winners.

By the way, the start of this week is also called, Kiss and Make Up Day. Take the time to forgive a friend and truly forgive and forget anything they have done!

August 26: For National Dog Day, watch your favorite dog movie - Benji, 101 Dalmations, and Spot. Read books, such as, *Clifford* and *Because of Winn-Dixie*. Revisit the animal shelter that you have been volunteering surprise them with homemade dog biscuits for the animals at the shelter. (This can be your random act of kindness)

Ingredients

2 eggs
1/2 cup canned pumpkin
2 tablespoons dry milk
1/4 teaspoon sea salt
2 1/2 cups brown rice flour *
1 teaspoon dried parsley (optional)

Directions

Preheat oven to 350°

In large bowl, whisk together eggs and pumpkin to smooth. Stir in dry milk, sea salt, and dried parsley (if using, optional). Add brown rice flour gradually, combining with spatula or hands to form a stiff, dry dough. Turn out onto lightly floured surface (can use the brown rice flour) and if dough is still rough, briefly knead and press to combine.

Roll dough flat and use a cookie cutter to make shapes. Bake 20 minutes. Remove from oven and carefully turn biscuits over, then bake additional 20 minutes. Allow to cool completely on rack before feeding to dog.

* Brown rice flour gives the biscuits crunch and promotes better dog digestion. Many dogs have touchy stomachs or allergies and do not tolerate wheat.

August 27: Make a homemade volcano and watch movies, such as, Volcano and Dante's Peak! Add cocoa powder to the baking soda or chocolate extract to the vinegar to make it a chocolate explosion. (Don't forget your random act of kindness)

August 28: Collect different types of magazines, be sure to include a few of your favorites. Use a large poster board to make a collage of what you would like to have in your life 10 or 20 years from that day. When I made mine I was sure to include an angel in the corner. It was to symbolize that if I was no longer alive, that I would continue to watch over my children. (Don't forget your random act of kindness)

August 29: Learn some of the basic words of American Sign language. (Don't forget your random act of kindness)

August 30: Today is Toasted Marshmallow Day! Have a bonfire with friends and family. Remember s'mores, hot dogs and of course, the marshmallows! (Don't forget your random act of kindness)

August 31: It's National Trail Mix Day! Get a collection of jars, a large bowl and your favorite treats! Make trail mix for your friends, a local daycare center or revisit the animal shelter and this time gifting the workers with your homemade trail mix for everything that they do! Make sundaes and sprinkle your trail mix on top! Enjoy them while you watch your favorite movie. (Don't forget your random act of kindness)

SEPTEMBER

September 1: Spend the day riding go-carts at a nearby track.

September 2: Happy Labor Day! This is the workers day to be acknowledged! Talk about what you do at your job. Then ask your children what they want to be when they grow up. Take time to learn about their dreams. Write about this day in your journal.

September 3: Use notebooks to make sticker books with all the stickers that you saved over the months.

September 4: For Newspaper Carrier Day, visit a newsstand and purchase several papers, if possible, seek newspapers from large cities, as well. It will be interesting to see the different styles of writing and to see what events are happening around you – far and wide.

Cut out the different comics and save your favorites in your Adventure Box.

September 5: For Cheese Pizza Day, make a homemade pizza! Use a variety of cookie cutters to make mini pizzas in different shapes. A fun book to read today is *Pizza at Sally's*.

September 6: Make plans to start a book club to celebrate Read a Book Day.

September 7: This is Classical Music Month. Introduce your children to Beethoven and Mozart – and even the Phantom of the Opera.

September 8: For Grandparent's Day, make a scrapbook to honor your grandparents, great-grandparents and even your great-grandparents

September 9: Teddy Bear Day! Visit your local Build-a-Bear Shop!

September 10: Today is Swap Ideas Day! Spend the day with friends that have the same hobbies as you. Share what activities you have been up to and swap ideas to encourage you both!

September 11: Honor those who passed away on 9/11 and those who continue the battle against terrorism. Make a care package for a platoon in the Middle East. Add plenty of homemade crafts – the soldiers use them to decorate.

September 12: Spend National Video Games Day at a local arcade, then make a trip to Dave and Buster's. When you get home watch Wreck it Ralph while you color images of Pac man and Super Mario that you download from Google.

September 13: It's Fortune Cookie Day! Have lunch at a Chinese restaurant and make strips of paper with your own fortunes on them for your friends.

September 14: For Square Dancing Month, attend a square dancing event! If you are brave enough, take a class! Contact the Happy Go Lucky Square Dance Club for information on this.

September 15: Spend the day at the Renaissance Fair.

September 16: Start your Mayflower Day with learning how Americans lived in the 1700's. Then start tracing your own family tree and learn all of your family's interesting stories. It will be fascinating to see how far your family has come.

September 17: This is Chicken Month! Visit a local chicken farm. Feed the chickens and learn fun facts of these feathered friends. When you get home, read *Henny Penny, Chicken Little*, and *Too Many Chickens*. Also, on this day, enjoy the movie, Chicken Run.

Have fun doing the Chicken Dance!

September 18: Learn about the Hispanic culture for Hispanic Heritage Month. Learn about Hispanics who made a difference in the world.

September 19: Celebrate "International Talk Like a Pirate Day" with a movie night of Pirates of the Caribbean or Jake and the Pirates. Make the day fun by dressing up as a pirate and having a treasure hunt. Fill a bin with sand and hide treasures deep inside to be found.

September 20: This is National Punch Day, as well as, POW/MIA Recognition Day. Make a bowl of punch (or 2 or 3) and a meat/cheese tray. Have friends over to watch your favorite war movies. Before and after each movie have a moment of silence for the MIA/POW soldiers.

Cherry Orange Punch:

6 cups water
2 cans (12 oz. Each) frozen Orange Juice
¾ cup Maraschino Cherry Juice
¾ cup sugar
1 liter Ginger Ale

Combine water, Orange Juice, Cherry Juice and sugar. Chill. Add Ginger Ale before serving.

Visit Allrecipes.com for a variety of punch recipes.

September 21: Celebrate International Rabbit Day by reading books, such as The Velveteen Rabbit, The Runaway Bunny and Peter Rabbit. Eat carrot cake and carrot sticks while you watch "Hop" and "Who Framed Roger Rabbit."

September 22: For Elephant Appreciation Day, visit the elephants at the zoo. Make a stop at the library to check out books about elephants and even the beloved Babar. When you get home watch the beloved movie, "Dumbo!" Make it more fun with a few games of Elefun!!

September 23: It's Checkers Day! Get a checkerboard cake from your favorite bakery and spend the afternoon playing Checkers with your friends. Put a twist to your Checker's Day by playing Chinese Checkers.

PS: You may have to order the checker cake in advance.

September 24: Celebrate the beginning of Autumn by revisiting the places you took photos on March 20th. Take more photos to add to your album of seasonal photos.

September 25: For National Comic Book Day, visit a few comic book shops and reconnect with a childhood favorite or find something new to read. Try making your own comic book too!

A fun superhero movie for the family to watch is The Incredibles.

September 26: In honor of Better Breakfast Month, host a dinner with a breakfast theme – serve only breakfast foods, like, coffee cake, different types of eggs, pop tarts, waffles, pancakes, french toast (with different syrups and tops), bacon, sausage, hash browns and more. The guests wear pajamas and everyone curls under their favorite blanket watching cartoons. Enjoy reading the Dr. Seuss book, *Scrambled Eggs Super.*

September 27: It is Native American Day, learn about the history of Native Americans. Visit the local library for books and documentaries.

September 28: Acknowledge National Good Neighbor Day and make cupcakes as a measure of friendship for your neighbors that you know the least.

September 29: For National Piano Month, take a few piano lessons and learn to play a song on the piano. Listen to the great piano music of such musicians as, Bach and Beethoven to Stevie Wonder, Billy Joel and Elton John.

September 30: Make this an angel day in honor of Nicholas Matthew Richards. He suffered birth defects and lived for only 18 days. Volunteer with Angel Wings from the Heart, cutting and gluing sequins and lace onto gowns and layette gifts that they make for preemies in the NICU.

OCTOBER

October 1: The first day of October marks the beginning of Get Organized Week. Make a bowl of Monster Juice – a combination of pineapple juice, lime juice, and ginger ale. Enjoy your monster juice while you clean out your closet or your favorite room.

October 2: This is also the beginning of Cookie Month. Make 2 or 3 types of cookies that you never made. Snack on your cookies while you watch, "Hocus Pocus."

October 3: Visit a pumpkin patch to pick up pumpkins for your fall decorations. Pick up several mini pumpkins too. Carve your new pumpkins into jack-o-lanterns and bake pumpkin seeds. With your mini pumpkins paint faces and designs on them.

October 4: Get ready for Halloween by making a tray of candy/caramel apples. Enjoy them while you watch, "It's the Great Pumpkin Charlie Brown" and "The Nightmare Before Christmas."

October 5: Learn about Halloween traditions and the different ways that people celebrate.

October 6: Today is Mad Hatter Day. Spend the day either reading the book "Alice in Wonderland" or watching the movie (or even both). Then make your own story (in your journal) about the fantasy world that you would find if you fell in the rabbit hole!

October 7: For Computer Learning Month take a lesson from your "computer whiz" friend. If that "computer whiz" is you, then give a lesson to a friend. Build your own website!

October 8: This is Fire Prevention Week, test your smoke alarms and map out your home's emergency escape routes. Finish the night by making a pot of chicken and dumplings. While you enjoy your meal, watch the movie Fireproof! Finish the night reading *Pickles the Fire Cat*.

October 9: For Curious Events Day, go to a book store/library and look up books of curious facts! Jot down your favorite ones in your journal. Test your curiosity by playing Guess Who and the card game.

October 10: Today is National Angel Food Cake Day! Make this sweet dessert for a snack while you watch the movie, Angels in the Outfield.

October 11: This is "It's My Party Day!" The best way to celebrate is by playing the 60's favorite, "It's My Party" song by Lesley Gore. Make this day a 60's Day! Listen to 60's music and watch 60's shows, such as, the Munsters, Bewitched, and Happy Days.

Snack on Jello Jigglers while you play with popular toys from the 60's, such as, Parchesi, viewmasters, slinkies, yo-yo's, Barbie dolls, and even a game (or two) of Trouble.

October 12: For Cookbook Launch Day, make a homemade cookbook with your favorite recipes – and even a few new ones that you want to try! Put the pages inside a photo album and make it your Family Holiday cookbook.

October 13: To combat the belief that "13" is an unlucky number, decorate "lucky horseshoes" to pass out to friends. Enjoy a delicious bowl Lucky Charms while you research fun superstitions and save your favorite ones in your journal.

October 14: For Columbus Day, tour a history museum and observe the time line of this country's history.

October 15: Make this a scary day! Take a walk through a haunted house. Finish the night with a haunted hayride!

October 16: For Apple Jack Month invite friends over to play Apples to Apples. Serve apple juice, apple chicken quesadillas, vanilla ice cream topped with crushed apple jacks and trail mix loaded with apple jacks!

October 17: For Clergy Appreciation Month, gift your reverend/priest with homemade cupcakes and a handwritten letter of "Thanks." Make edible glitter to sprinkle on top of your cupcakes. To make edible glitter, mix ¼ cup sugar and a ½ teaspoon food coloring. Spread across a baking pan and bake at 350 degrees for 10 minutes.

October 18: Decorate pumpkin cookies with candy corn. Snack on your cookies while you make a Halloween banner for your bedroom wall.

October 19: The third Saturday of October is Sweetest Day! Show your love to your friends, your partner or even your "secret love." Here are some ways to show the people that you care about that they are "the sweetest"

October 20: Listen to Halloween songs like "The Monster Mash" and "Purple People Eater" while you make a mini scrapbook of your favorite Halloween images.

October 21: Take a walk through a corn field maze. While you are there, pick up fresh ears of corn to accompany a barbecue in the evening.

October 22: Make Halloween crafts! With construction paper, cut out the shapes that you need to make a jack-o-lantern. Make a black cat by painting a paper plate black and gluing on wiggly eyes, a pink nose, whiskers and yellow smile. Decorate pillowcase to use for trick-or-treating on Halloween.

October 23: Have a day of ghosts! Make ghost cookies by dipping Nutter Butter cookies in white chocolate and use mini chocolate chips for the eyes. Watch Casper while you make ghosts. Glue cotton balls to ghost shapes and hang them from the ceiling. Make a ghost windsock by using white streamers and painting a paper towel/toilet paper holder.

October 24: During International Drum Month, learn about famous drummers, their lives and their triumphs. Have lunch at the Hard Rock Cafe.

Make your own drums by snipping off the tip of a balloon and stretching it across a tin can. Hold it down by wrapping a gum band around it.

October 25: For World Pasta Day make this a healthy homemade day! Make spaghetti with homemade spaghetti sauce, homemade meatballs, homemade bread and homemade butter! Have salad with vegetables from the garden and your favorite homemade dessert. For fun, watch "Cloudy with a Chance of Meatballs," after dinner.

Teach your children the song, "On Top of Spaghetti!"

October 26: It was on this day that Doc Holiday and the Earp Brothers engaged in the shoot-out at the OK Corral. Make this a Cowboy Day! Decorate your home to look like the old west. Watch "Tombstone" (with Val Kilmer and Kurt Russell) and for lunch eat hot dogs and baked beans; using a metal pie pan for your plate. Make "Cactus Juice" by mixing lime sherbet, 7Up and limeade or lemon lime Kool-aid! Also, make Haystack Cookies (these are no-bake cookies)

NO BAKE' HAYSTACK COOKIES

2 cups (12 oz) semisweet chocolate chips
2 cups butterscotch chips (or peanut butter if no allergies)
½ tsp. vanilla
3 cups chow mien noodles
Optional: May add 1 cup chopped walnuts or peanuts.

Melt chips; mix in noodles until coated well.
Drop by teaspoon onto was paper. Put in refrigerator to set.

October 27: Play a game of "Pumpkin Bowling!" With a black marker, make ghost faces on rolls of toilet paper – these are your bowling pins. You can arrange them together or stack them in a pattern. Get a small pumpkin to use as the bowling ball. Remember to cut the stem off first.

October 28: For Plush Animal Lover's Day, revisit the Build-a-Bear workshop. Make a stuffed animal – other than the teddy bear! When you get home watch the Toy Story movies 1-3 with your new stuffed friend.

October 29: Make it an old scary movies day! Play homage to the classics of Frankenstein, The Birds and Psycho!

October 30: Now opt for a modern day scarefest with your favorite scary movies – Friday the 13th, Poltergeist, Nightmare on Elm Street, and of course, Halloween!

October 31: Have a Halloween party with a few friends or cousins. Here are fun games to play at your party.

*Fill a fish bowl with candy corn and see who can guess how many are inside the bowl.

*Create a Mummy Bowling game. Wrap your plastic bowling pins in gauze tape and decorate them with black eyes that you cut prom construction paper or electrical tape.

*Play a Halloween Word Race Game. Set a timer for one minute and everyone writes down as many Halloween related words that they can think of. The one with the most words wins a prize or a small bag of candy treats.

*Play a pumpkin toss game. Wrap orange paper around a metal can and decorate the face of a pumpkin. Make simple bean bags with fabric swatches sewn together and filled with rice or beans. Toss the bean bags into the can, the one scoring the most points wins a small price or candy bag. You can make more than one can and space them out on the floor – each one being worth more points.

Make a trail mix of, candy corn, Frankenberry or Count Chocula cereal, pretzels, and mini marshmallows. Also, make a plate of hamburgers and pass them out to the police officers and firefighters on patrol!

Recipe for a fun Halloween Punch:

Ingredients

1 can (46 ounces) pineapple juice, divided
1 package (3 ounces) orange gelatin
1 carton (64 ounces) orange juice
1 liter ginger ale, chilled
1 quart orange sherbet

Directions

In a saucepan, bring 1 cup of pineapple juice to a boil. Stir in gelatin until dissolved. Cool; transfer to a large pitcher or container. Add orange juice and remaining pineapple juice. Chill. Just before serving, pour into a punch bowl; add ginger ale and mix well. Top with scoops of sherbet.

NOVEMBER

November 1: November is known as Nanowrimo. That stands for National Novel Writing Month. Do you have an idea for a book that you always wanted to write? Now is a great time to do that!

November 2: Go sled riding at a nearby winter resort.

November 3: For Sandwich Day, invite friends/family over for a sandwich bake-off. Make your own creative sandwiches – hot or cold!

November 4: Celebrate King Tut Day by learning the history of King Tut and watching movies like, "The Mummy" and "The Curse of King Tut's Tomb."

November 5: Take a pottery class. Make an extra cherished piece for someone in a nursing home who doesn't get any visitors.

November 6: Talk about the pilgrims and Native Americans at that first Thanksgiving. Read books about the families from that cold harsh year!

Did you know that the first Thanksgiving was actually 3 days long and they did not eat turkey?

Did you know that the Macy's Day parade was started by immigrants working at Macy's, who wanted to celebrate their new American heritage.

Potatoes were not served at the first Thanksgiving. Irish immigrants had not brought them over yet.

November 7: Spend the day at the Ringling Brother's Circus.

November 8: Get a blender, your favorite juice drinks and a bowl of ice to make homemade snow cones. Enjoy your snow cones while you watch the movie Frozen. You can make your own snow cone syrup. Mix 2 cups sugar and 3/4 cups water and heat till sugar dissolves. Add your favorite unsweetened Kool-aid. Store in fridge. Pour over finely crushed ice.

Paint your own snowman pictures and make it more fun by making Olaf Paint. To make Olaf Paint, mix equal parts of shaving cream and white glue. Sprinkle the mixture with blue glitter.

November 9: Make a Thanksgiving Day banner. Fill it with photos for your family, even ones from long ago or ones that have moved away. Add hearts, stickers, drawings and fun messages.

November 10: Have a classic movie night. Watch movies like, Casablanca, Gone with the Wind and Guess Who's Coming to Dinner.

November 11: To honor the fallen soldiers this Veteran's Day, attend a local parade and thank the soldiers in attendance for their service as well. Write thank you cards and deliver them to a nearby American Legion.

November 12: Today is Chicken Soup for the Soul Day! Go to the library to check out your favorite chicken soup books! When you get home, read your books over a bowl of homemade chicken soup.

November 13: For Go Caroling Day, listen to Christmas music and sing Christmas carols. Listen to some Christmas songs that you haven't heard before. End the day, watching the movie, "Prancer."

November 14: November 14th has been donned American Teddy Bear Day.

It was in November of 1902 when Teddy Roosevelt took a hunting trip with his friends and refused to shoot a bear that they held captive to make the hunt easier for him. He said it took away from the sport of hunting and he had the young bear released into the wild. A reporter made a comic mimicking the trip and named the bear, "Teddy's Bear." When a toy store owner saw the comic he made stuffed animals in the likeliness of the bear – this became known as the Teddy Bear.

Read your favorite bear books – the Berenstain Bears, Corduroy, or even Little Bear. Also, have fun singing the children's song, Going on a Bear Hunt.

November 15: Make place mats for your Thanksgiving dinner. Color downloaded images or make your own pictures on construction paper. Laminate them to create place mats. Make one for each family member.

On the back of each place mat fill in this sentence, "I admire _____ because..."

November 16: To commemorate Harry Potter Day, hold a marathon of Harry Potter movies and share your favorite parts of the book!

November 17: Make a variety of breads for Homemade Bread Day! Some flavors of bread are German Sweet Bread, Wheat, Chocolate, Banana, Zucchini, Pumpernickel and Cherry Bread! Also use some of the bread dough to make biscuits and bread sticks.

November 18: For Game and Puzzle Week, invite friends over for a Game Night of board games, such as, Sorry, Monopoly, Connect 4, Life, Scattergories, and the Logo Board Game.

November 19: Today is National Have a Bad Day! Celebrate with a day of pandemonium! Start the day off wearing mismatched clothes – especially socks! Watch the movie, "Jingle All the Way" and read the books *Alexander and the Terrible, Horrible, No Good, Very Bad Day* and *Mean Soup*. The best part of this crazy day is playing a few games of Chutes & Ladders.

Make a Butterfingers dip by mixing an 8 ounce pack of cream cheese, 4 ounces of cool whip, and a 10 ounce jar of marshmallow cream. Chop up 10 bite sized Butterfingers and add them to the mixture. (Or you can use 3 full size Butterfingers) Serve your dip with fruit slices, pretzels or Nilla wafers.

November 20: Build an igloo from sugar cubes. Then play a few games of Don't Break the Ice.

November 21: Play Thanksgiving Memory. Cut a stack of squares from construction paper and attach Thanksgiving stickers in pairs of "cards." Use these cards to play Memory.

November 22: Watch A Charlie Brown Thanksgiving! In the meantime, cook some of your Thanksgiving dishes early and freeze them. This will save time on Thanksgiving Day.

November 23: Talk to your relatives – as many as possible – and learn a few facts about everyone. Put it together into a book titles "FUN FAMILY FACTS" and send copies to everyone for Christmas!

November 24: Happy Thanksgiving! Celebrate with your friends and family. Have each person bring 3 things to the table that they are thankful for, even if it is a photo of the important people in their life. In lieu of place cards, put a fun photo in your guest's seating place. Play a game of Memory Sharing with your family on Thanksgiving. Fill a glass jar with strips of paper with random questions. Each person pulls a piece from the jar and answers it honestly. Write the best answers in your journal. Suggestions:

*My favorite childhood toy.

*My first experience eating food from another country.

*The best thing that happened this year.

*My most embarrassing moment.

November 25: For National Parfait Day, make parfaits – anyway you like...add toppings of your choice! You can also make your own ice cream in a bag.

1 small ziploc bag
1 large ziploc bag
1 tablespoon sugar
1/2 cup milk
1/4 teaspoon vanilla
6 tablespoon salt

In each small bag add the milk, vanilla, & sugar; seal the bag. Fill the large bag half full with ice; add salt. Place the small bag inside the large bag and seal. Shake until mixture is the consistency of ice cream takes about 5 minutes.

Enjoy your treat while you watch Home Alone. Take a break from turkey today and make English Muffin pizzas. Topping each with sauce, cheese, and your favorite toppings.

November 26: Bake your favorite cake for Cake Day. Take a slice of cake to your librarian and look up books like *Just Grace and the Trouble with Cupcakes*, and *Amelia Bedelia Bakes Off*.

November 27: Celebrate Pins and Needles Day by making friendship pins and decorative pins. Pass them out to friends and family on Thanksgiving!

November 28: Learn winter survival skills. Learn about disaster preparedness and make a "black-out kit" for your home! A black-out kit is a box or basket filled with candles, flashlights, batteries, candles and matches. So, if your electric goes out, you have everything you need in one place. Here are some tips: Buy a box of birthday candles. Use the birthday candles to light all the others. If you turn a funnel upside down it makes a great candlestick holder (use the metal ones, not plastic). They even have a handle!

November 29: Do you have leftover mashed potatoes? Make mashed potato balls!

Made a ball of potatoes around a cube of cheese. Roll them in potato chips. Bake at 350 degrees until light brown.

November 30: Make a list of activity ideas to celebrate advent in December. Use them to make an advent calendar.

DECEMBER

December 1: Today is Faith Crusenberry Day. She is a victim of bullying in the schools. Visit the "Faith Crusenberry Foundation" facebook page and page homage to this sweet soul. In honor of Faith, talk to your child about bullies and the impact that they can have. Bullies are not the same as they were 20 years ago – they are more violent. Teach your child the warning signs and how they can keep themselves safe. And watch movies, such as, "Tuff Turf," "Cyber Bully" or "You Again." Some books about bullies for younger children include *Stand Tall, Molly Lou Melon*, and *The Recess Queen*. Books for older children include, *Hate List*, and *By the Time You Read This, I'll Be Dead*.

When you log onto the Faith Crusenberry Foundation page be sure to order your Faith bracelet and show the world that your family does not tolerate bullying of any kind.

December 2: Get a stack of construction paper and markers and make signs for friends and family. Also, hang up signs for a bake sale – it's your activity on the 9th. To further help your bake sale, you can advertise for free through your local churches and by hanging signs in the grocery store.

December 3: For Bingo Month have a day of Bingo games. Each person attending brings a roll of quarters and several small inexpensive gifts, (pot holders, magnets, key chains, candles, small books, mug, and more). They have to wrap the gifts also. The winner of each game gets a few quarters and a wrapped gift.

December 4: Learn about the Christmas traditions of the different nationalities. Take notes in your journal!

December 5: Make gingerbread man cookies. Enjoy them while you read *The Gingerbread Man* and watch the movie, Shrek. ("Not my gumdrop buttons!") By the way, if you turn the gingerbread men upside down you can make Reindeer cookies.

December 6: For Mitten Tree Day, cut mittens out of construction paper or card stock. Decorate them and add messages of hope, love and thanks! Deliver them to the children at Auberle or a nearby women's shelter.

December 7: Spend the day baking cookies and cupcakes for your bake sale the next day.

December 8: It's bake sale day! Have a bake sale and juice stand and use the money for a special surprise for children in the hospital. When you get home, make homemade Christmas cards for tomorrow's activity. With the money from your bake sale, pick up the small gifts you will be delivering.

December 9: This is Christmas Card Day! Deliver your Christmas cards to children in the hospital. Include a candy cane, a sheet of stickers, a pen and a small notebook.

December 10: Have a Reindeer Day! Start the day by reading "Rudolph the Red-Nosed Reindeer." Make reindeer by gluing craft sticks into a triangle. Decorate with googly eyes and a red pom pom for the nose. If you want, you can use a marker to color the craft sticks brown.

Now that you read the book, watch the movie "Rudolph the Red Nosed Reindeer," snack on reindeer chow, make from a mixture of bugles, pretzel sticks, red and white M&M's, shredded wheat, and chocolate chips.

December 11: Gather craft supplies and make homemade Christmas Tree ornaments.

December 12: Winter is here – it's time for big sweaters, snowballs, and FROSTY THE SNOWMAN!

Make a snowman for the window with shapes cut out of construction paper. You can also make snowman bookmarks by painting Popsicle sticks white, and use wiggly eyes and buttons to create a snowman. Wrap a ribbon around for the scarf. Use a triangular piece of orange felt/paper for the nose. Make a black hat from either a ball of tissue paper or a piece of construction paper. You can also turn your bookmark into an ornament.

Finish your snowy day with watching Frosty the Snowman.

December 13: Have fun celebrating the National Day of the Horse. Pick up books about horses and note your favorite facts in your journal. Finish the night off watching movies like, Spirit and National Velvet. A fun book to read with your children is, *The Artist Who Painted a Blue Horse*. There is even a board game from that same book. Or play the "My Horse Show" board game.

December 14: Visit the Christmas light displays throughout your community or a nearby town and take photos. Then decorate wooden or foam frames from your local craft store. Fill the picture frames with photos you took and give them to friends and family as Christmas gifts.

December 15: Celebrate National Lemon Cupcake Day by making these tasty treats! Top with vanilla/butter cream frosting and pieces of fresh fruit. Make glasses of homemade lemonade to go with them! Deliver a few cupcakes – and some homemade Christmas cards - to a nearby VFW or American Legion.

December 16: This is National Chocolate Covered Anything Day! Have a chocolate fondue lunch. To dip in your chocolate fondue, prepare cut up pieces of fruit, sponge cake and marshmallows.

December 17: Make a batch of Christmas Coal while you watch, "The Grinch that Stole Christmas." To make Christmas Coal you need 4 cups of rice cereal, ¼ cup butter, 10 ounce bag of mini marshmallows, and 1/8 teaspoon black food coloring.

In a large pot melt the butter and gradually add the marshmallows. Continue stirring until the marshmallows are melted. Add the food coloring, and last the rice cereal. Shape into pieces of coal.

December 18: Make Snowman Soup: A bowl of melted vanilla ice cream, ½ cup of milk, a dash of vanilla, pretzel pieces, fresh fruit, peanuts and chocolate chips. Enjoy your Snowman Soup while you watch, Frosty the Snowman and read *The Snowy Day* (Ezra Jack Keats).

December 19: Spend the day watching Christmas Movies. Here are some ideas:

Home Alone
Polar Express
It's a Wonderful Life
Miracle on 34th Street
A Christmas Carol
A Charlie Brown Christmas

December 20: For Go Caroling Day, listen to Christmas music and sing Christmas carols for residents at a nursing home. Make a list of your favorite Christmas songs in your journal. Also, list 10 things you love about winter and your top 10 favorite Christmas memories! Finish the day by watching, "Prancer!"

December 21: Today is the first day of winter. Revisit the places you took photos for on March 20th. Take plenty of photos to complete your seasonal photos album. Take note of how the trees change with the seasons.

December 22: Make a Family Christmas Story. Write the first 2 pages of a winter/Christmas adventure book. Over the next year ahead, contact each family member and have each one write a piece of the book. For example, one of your cousin's can write pages 3 & 4, a sibling can write pages 5 & 6, etc. Before it ends, you can write the last 2 pages. Take your time, give yourself the whole year to complete the book. At Christmas time next year, make a copy of the book for each person that helped contribute!

December 23: Make a candy Christmas tree for the centerpiece at your Christmas dinner. To do this you will need a cone shaped ice cream come, green and white frosting, and candy pieces.

Step 1: Spread white frosting on your plate. This will symbolize snow!

Step 2: Turn the cone upside-down and set it in the middle of the frosting to symbolize a tree.

Step 3: Cover the tree with green frosting. Your child can use a spoon to do that part.

Step 4: Decorate with candy pieces.

December 24: Attend a Christmas Eve service. If you don't celebrate Christmas, then take this time to appreciate the holiday of your beliefs.

At night, sprinkle reindeer food in your yard to help Santa find the way! Make reindeer food by mixing ¼ Cup oatmeal, ¼ Cup sugar, red and green sugar crystals or glitter.

December 25: Forgive anyone of ill feelings that you are holding onto and show your love and appreciation to the important people in your life! Never let them forget how important they are! In your journal, write about the peace that you have made with others.

December 26: Make an "About Me" scrapbook. Make one for each person in your family!

December 27: Today is National Cut Out Snowflakes Day! Start the day by making a tray of No Bake Snowballs, to enjoy later.

Ingredients

1 8-ounce Cream Cheese (softened)
1 8-ounce can of crushed pineapples (drain well)
1 Cup chopped pecans
3 Cups of Flaked Coconut

Combine cream cheese & pineapples. Fold in pecans. Cover & Refrigerate for 1 hour. Roll into 1" balls. Roll in coconut. Refrigerate for 4 hours.

While you wait for the snowballs, cut out a variety of paper snowflakes to decorate your windows. Take a few snowflakes to your favorite small business owner! When you get home, enjoy your snowballs while you watch the movie, Snow Day.

December 28: Make this an afternoon of card games to celebrate National Card Playing Day! Play Go Fish, Gin, Spades, Old Maid, Memory, and, of course, Uno. Try building a house of cards too! Watch the movie, "21," with older children.

December 29: Go Ice Skating at a local skating rink.

December 30: Make your own list of activities for the new year! Start a blog and share the days and your experiences with others. Make a new Activity Box for all of next year's adventures!

December 31: Happy New Year! On this night have a "Toast to a Change" with your friends and family. During the toast, you can each say something that you want to change or do in the upcoming year! Something other than dieting or quitting smoking!

Before the night is over, review the list you made on January 11th and see how many of your goals you achieved! Dive into the items you saved in your Activity Box. Write the last pages of your journal and reflect on the past year – the good and the bad!

Things I Want to Try Next Year

Other titles from Higher Ground Books & Media:

Wise Up to Rise Up by Rebecca Benston

A Path to Shalom by Steen Burke

From a Hole in My Life to a Life Made Whole by Janet Kay Teresa

Overcomer by Forrest Henslee

Miracles: I Love Them by Forest Godin

32 Days with Christ's Passion by Mark Etter

The Magic Egg by Linda Phillipson

The Tin Can Gang by Chuck David

Whobert the Owl by Mya C. Benston

Dear You by Derra Nicole Sabo

For His Eyes Only by John Salmon, PhD

Add these titles to your collection today!

http://highergroundbooksandmedia.com

www.ingramcontent.com/pod-product-compliance
Lightning Source LLC
Chambersburg PA
CBHW022119280326
41933CB00007B/461